First World War
and Army of Occupation
War Diary
France, Belgium and Germany

37 DIVISION
112 Infantry Brigade
Hertfordshire Regiment
1 Battalion
1 May 1918 - 31 March 1919

WO95/2537/2

The Naval & Military Press Ltd
www.nmarchive.com
Published in association with The National Archives

Published by

The Naval & Military Press Ltd

Unit 10 Ridgewood Industrial Park,
Uckfield, East Sussex,
TN22 5QE England
Tel: +44 (0) 1825 749494

www.naval-military-press.com

www.nmarchive.com

This diary has been reprinted in facsimile from the original. Any imperfections are inevitably reproduced and the quality may fall short of modern type and cartographic standards.

© **Crown Copyright**
Images reproduced by permission of The National Archives, London, England, 2015.

Contents

Document type	Place/Title	Date From	Date To
Heading	WO95/2537/2		
Heading	37th Division 112th Infy Bde 1st Bn Herts Regt 1918 Feb-Mar 1919 From 39 Div 118 Bde		
Heading	War Diary Of 1st. Bn. Hertfordshire Regt. From 1st May 1918 To 31st May 1918 (Volume 43)		
War Diary		01/05/1918	31/05/1918
Heading	War Diary Of 1st Battalion The Hertfordshire Regiment. For The Month Of June 1918 Vol 43		
War Diary		05/06/1918	25/06/1918
Heading	War Diary Of 1st Battalion The Hertfordshire Regiment For The Month Of July 1918		
War Diary		03/07/1918	28/07/1918
Heading	War Diary Of 1/1 Hertfordshire Regt For Month Of August 1918 Volume XC VIII.		
War Diary	Trenches.	01/08/1918	01/08/1918
War Diary	Souastre	02/08/1918	09/08/1918
War Diary	Trenches	09/08/1918	31/08/1918
Heading	War Diary Of 1st Bn The Hertfordshire Regiment For The Month Of September 1918 Vol 47		
War Diary		01/09/1918	30/09/1918
Miscellaneous	The Military Cross.		
Heading	War Diary Of 1st. Bn. The Hertfordshire Regiment For The Month Of October 1918 Volume		
War Diary		01/10/1918	31/10/1918
Miscellaneous	During the Month the following Awards were Announced		
Miscellaneous	Bar To The Military Medal.	31/10/1918	31/10/1918
Heading	War Diary Of 1st Bn. The Hertfordshire Regt. For November 1918 Vol 49		
War Diary		01/11/1918	22/11/1918
Operation(al) Order(s)	Operation Order No. 6	02/11/1918	02/11/1918
Operation(al) Order(s)	In Continuation of Operation Order No. 6	03/11/1918	03/11/1918
Miscellaneous		03/11/1918	03/11/1918
Heading	War Diary Of 1st Battn. The Hertfordshire Regt For The Month Of December 1918 Vol 50		
War Diary		01/12/1918	31/12/1918
Miscellaneous	Return Shewing Decrease In Strength For The Month Of December 1918	09/01/1919	09/01/1919
Heading	1/1st Bn. Hertfordshire Regt. War Diary. Volume LI January, 1919		
War Diary		00/01/1919	00/01/1919
Miscellaneous	Bn to the Military Crops.		
Miscellaneous	Return Shewing Decrease In Strength For The Month Of January 1919		
Heading	War Diary Of 1/1st Bn The Hertfordshire Regt. For The Month Of February 1919 Volume 52		
Miscellaneous	Headquarters, 112th Infantry Brigade.	28/02/1919	28/02/1919
War Diary		00/02/1919	28/02/1919
Miscellaneous	Return Shewing Decrease In Strength For The Month Of February 1919		

| War Diary | Ransart. | 01/03/1919 | 10/03/1919 |
| War Diary | Jumet. | 11/03/1919 | 31/03/1919 |

W095/25371/2

37TH DIVISION
112TH INFY BDE

1ST BN HERTS REGT

~~MAY 1918~~-MAR 1919

1918 FEB

FROM { 39 DIV
       118 Bde

CONFIDENTIAL

WAR DIARY

OF

1ST. BN. HERTFORDSHIRE REGT.

From 1st May 1918 to 31st May 1918

(VOLUME 43)

WAR DIARY
or
INTELLIGENCE SUMMARY.

Army Form C. 2118.

Place	Date	Hour	Summary of Events and Information	Remarks and references to Appendices
May. 1918.				
	May 1st.		The Bn. moved into reserve at Café Belge.	
	2nd.		The Bn. moved back to a camp at BRANDHOEK.	
	3rd.		The Bn. moved to TUNNELLING CAMP — Situated on the POPERINGHE - WATOU Road.	
	4th.		The Bn. marched to CROMBEEKE and entrained for AUDRICQ, arriving at AUDRICQ at about 3 am. on May 5th.	
	5th.		Bn. arrived in billets at NIELLES LES ARDRES about 7 a.m. General reorganising & re-equipping of Bn.	
	6th. & 7th.			
	8th.		Bn. marched to AUDRICQ Station and entrained for CANDAS at 9 a.m. to transfer to the 37th Division. Bn. arrived at CANDAS during the afternoon and was conveyed by lorries to ORVILLE where the Bn. spent two nights in the open.	

WAR DIARY or INTELLIGENCE SUMMARY

Army Form C. 2118.

Place	Date	Hour	Summary of Events and Information	Remarks and references to Appendices
War	11.7		The Bn. entrained at ORVILLE at 5 pm and on detraining at SOUASTRE marched to some old British trenches East of FONQUEVILLERS. The Bn. on its move through the village of FONQUEVILLERS and into the old line of trenches East of the village was subjected to a very heavy gas shell bombardment. The Commanding Officer, Lieut. Col. R. WILKINSON DSO and the whole of the Officers with the exception of Captain N.P. GALD were evacuated to hospital during the night. All the NCO's and men with the exception of 7 men evacuated to hospital. Capt. N.P. GOLD and the remaining 7 O.R's returned to the transport the following morning (May 12th), and later in the day this Officer and 5 of the men who returned were evacuated to C.C.S.	
	13.7		The Bn. i.e. Transport, Q.M. Stores & Details moved to billets at LOUVENCOURT. A draft of 1 Officer (Captain S.W.MOORE and 81 O.R. joined the Bn.	

Army Form C. 2118.

WAR DIARY
or
INTELLIGENCE SUMMARY.
(Erase heading not required.)

Place	Date	Hour	Summary of Events and Information	Remarks and references to Appendices
May	22nd		The Bn. absorbed the 6th (S) Bn. Beatrachie Regt. (less Transport and Training Staff). Numbers absorbed – Officers 30, O. Ranks 650. Major R.C. CARTHEW, M.C. 1st Essex Regt assumed command of the Bn.	
"	23rd		The Bn. marched to a camp on the outskirts of the village of VAUCHELLES.	
"	24 6/30.		Bn. in Sluice training	
	3/6.		Bn. inspected by Brigadier-General A.E. IRVINE, D.S.O. Commanding 112th Infantry Brigade. The following message was received from H.Q. 112 Inf. Bde. "The Brigade Commander wishes to place on record his appreciation of the way in which your Battalion turned out"	

Army Form C. 2118.

WAR DIARY
or
INTELLIGENCE SUMMARY.
(Erase heading not required.)

Place	Date	Hour	Summary of Events and Information.	Remarks and references to Appendices
			In inspection to-day, in spite of the fact that the 1/1st HERTS Regt. has only quite recently been formed out of the remnants of two battalions, the rifle of all ranks was excellent, and did credit to the work done by all officers and N.C.O's during the last few weeks. It was a pleasure to the Brigade Commander to see the men's steadiness on parade. During the month, the following have been awarded decorations. The Military Cross. Lieut. C.B.G. Cripps. 2/Lieut. J.E. Rogers (late Bedf. Regt.) The Distinguished Conduct Medal. No. 265089 Sgt. H. Randall.	

WAR DIARY
or
INTELLIGENCE SUMMARY.
(Erase heading not required.)

Army Form C. 2118.

Place	Date	Hour	Summary of Events and Information	Remarks and references to Appendices
			Bar to Military Medal	
			N° 266265 Sgt. Clement, C.	
			The Military Medal	
			N° 265931 Sgt. G. Adam.	
			265476 Cpl. J. Ramsden.	
			266691 L/Cpl. J. Butterfield.	
			265908 L/C. B. Kent.	
			271492 Pte. C. Abrahams.	
			N.C.Patten Major.	
			Commanding 1/Kent. Regt.	

37/112

1st 43

War Diary
of
1st Battalion "The Hertfordshire Regiment"

For the month of

June 1918

Original.

WAR DIARY
or
INTELLIGENCE SUMMARY

(Erase heading not required.)

Army Form C. 2118.

Instructions regarding War Diaries and Intelligence Summaries are contained in F. S. Regs., Part II. and the Staff Manual respectively. Title Pages will be prepared in manuscript.

Place	Date	Hour	Summary of Events and Information	Remarks and references to Appendices
June	5/6/2		Bn moved by bus and march route to billets at Pissy, arriving in billets at about 4 a.m. on 6th.	
	6th & 10th		Bn. training at Pissy.	
		10th	Bn. proceeded by bus and march route to LAWARDE MAUGER, arriving in billets about 11 p.m.	
		13th	Bn. marched to billets in SAINS-EN-AMIENS, arriving in billets at 3 a.m on June 14th.	
		15th	Bn. marched to billets at St FUSCIEN.	
		20th	Bn. marched to billets at TAIGNI.	
	21/6/2		Bn. marched to LOSUILLY and entrained at 9 am for AUTHIEUX, the Bn. detrained at 3 pm & marched to billets at TERRAMES	

WAR DIARY
or
INTELLIGENCE SUMMARY

(Erase heading not required.)

Army Form C. 2118.

Place	Date	Hour	Summary of Events and Information	Remarks and references to Appendices
	June 26th		Bn. moved by bus to SOUASTRE and on detraining marched to reserve trenches East of FONQUEVILLERS.	
			During the month the following awards have been announced:-	
			The Military Cross	
			Captain A. G. GRINLING.	
			Captain J. F. CHRISTIE	
			Lieut. H. J. HENSMAN	
			The Distinguished Conduct Medal.	
			No 265216 Sgt. A. N. Allen.	
			Bar to the Military Medal.	
			No 266265 Sgt. G. Clements, M.M.	

WAR DIARY
or
INTELLIGENCE SUMMARY

Army Form C. 2118.

Place	Date	Hour	Summary of Events and Information	Remarks and references to Appendices
			The Military Medal.	
			No 265931. Sgt. G. Adams.	
			No 265908. Ye. B. Kent.	
			No 265474. Cpl. F. Ramsden.	
	30.6.18			

M. R. Matthew Major
Commanding 1st Bn. 12th Regt.

War Diary
of
1st Battalion The Hertfordshire Regiment
for the month of
July 1918.

… **WAR DIARY** or **INTELLIGENCE SUMMARY**
(Erase heading not required.)

Army Form C. 2118.

37/12

Vol L 3

Place	Date	Hour	Summary of Events and Information	Remarks and references to Appendices
	3.7.18		The Battalion moved from "Z" to support at PIGEON WOOD.	
	6.7.18		The Battalion took over front line in the Right Sub-sector.	
	12.7.18		The Battalion was raided by small party of the Enemy. One German remaining in our hands. Our casualties slight.	
	13.7.18		The Battalion was relieved and moved back to support at the "Z".	
	16.7.18		The Battalion was relieved by 10th Bn. Essex Regt, and moved to a camp at SOUASTRE.	
	20.7.18		The Battalion relieved the 1st Bn. Royal Fusiliers in the Right Sub-sector.	
	28.7.18		The Battalion was relieved and moved to support in the vicinity of ESSARTS.	
			During the month the undermentioned were awarded the Military Medal.	
			17263 Sgt. Currie J.	
			40481 Pte. Middleton A.	
			McCollom Lieut Col.	
			Commanding 10th Bn. The Bedfordshire Regiment.	

War Diary

of

1/1 Hertfordshire Regt

for Month of

August 1918

Volume XCVIII

WAR DIARY
or
INTELLIGENCE SUMMARY.
(Erase heading not required.)

Army Form C. 2118.

Instructions regarding War Diaries and Intelligence Summaries are contained in F. S. Regs., Part II. and the Staff Manual respectively. Title pages will be prepared in manuscript.

Place	Date	Hour	Summary of Events and Information	Remarks and references to Appendices
Trenches	1/8/18		Battn in Right sub-sector - Left section of Divisional front. (BUCQUOY)	
			Relieved night 1/2nd Aug & moved back to Divisional Reserve 2 Corps in CHATEAU-de-LA-HAIE Switch & two Coys nr HQ in SOUASTRE.	
Souastre	7/8/18	6		
Trenches	9/8/18		Battn in Billets in Souastre. Working parties found daily.	
	9/8/18		Battn moved to line Right Sub-sector Right Section (BUCQUOY).	
to	10/8/18	15	Battn in line - The enemy started a movement on the Right on the evening of 13th Aug - line was slightly pushed forward on	
	15/8/18		night 14/15th. Four prisoners captured.	
do	15/8/18		Battn relieved by 13th Yorks R Fusiliers & moved into support in PIGEON WOOD.	
	16/8/18	6		
	18/8/18		Battn in support. Working parties found daily.	
	18/8/18		Battn took over from 111th Bde in front line in ABLAINZEVELLE - BUCQUOY Sector.	
	20/8/18		Relieved in front line by Mk Bde & moved back to position of readiness	

WAR DIARY
or
INTELLIGENCE SUMMARY.
(Erase heading not required.)

Army Form C. 2118.

Place	Date	Hour	Summary of Events and Information	Remarks and references to Appendices
Irenches	21/8/18		in MISTY TRENCH. 11.K. Infl Rgt attacked at 4.55 pm. The Battn found carrying parties & working parties for Strong points. Battn moved back to trenches in support at 4.30 pm.	
	22/8/18		Battn resting in BRADFORD – LEEDS + HALIFAX TRENCHES. moved up to	
	23/8/18		assembly positions S. of LOG EAST. WOOD. at 11.0 pm. Battn attacked at 11.0 Am. Attack successful. Railway cutting in front of ACHIET LE GRAND taken. Casualties: Capt S.W. MOORE + 2 Lt./3 SMITH Killed. 7 Officers wounded. O.Ranks 26 Killed 140 wounded.	
	24/8/18		Battn moved to positions SE of BIHUCOURT.	
	25/8/18			
	31/8/18		Battn in divisional reserve in shelters SE of BIHUCOURT.	

McArthur Lt. Col.
Comdg 1st Bn Herts R.

War Diary
of
"1st. Bn. The Hertfordshire Regiment"
for the month of
September 1918

WAR DIARY
or
INTELLIGENCE SUMMARY
(Erase heading not required.)

Army Form C. 2118.

1/1 NZRB

Place	Date	Hour	Summary of Events and Information	Remarks and references to Appendices
September 1st 1918			Bn continued training at ACHIET LE GRAND.	
"	3rd		Bn. moved in morning to Edge of FAVREUIL Hut at 6.30 pm Set out to relieve 1st BEDS Regt. Relief completed 1.30 am	
"	4th		Coys moved forward to attack at 7 am. The New Zealand Div. who were advancing to our right did not assemble so far east as we did. Consequently we were not in touch with them when the Battalion advanced. At 9.30 am a report was received that the Battalion was held up by Machine Gun fire. Shortly after this N°3 Coy reported that this patrols had reached the wood in K.31.c and that the Coy was advancing behind its patrols. N°3 Coy reported enemy advancing in HAVRINCOURT and many of them seen working towards Guards wood in Q.2.c. The artillery was firing on Coys advancing point with unknown results. At 9 pm a runner from N°2 Coy who had been lost for a considerable time arrived and went back to the Coy and brought them back to Battalion H.Q. They had got mixed up with the New Zealand	

WAR DIARY
or
INTELLIGENCE SUMMARY.
(Erase heading not required.)

Army Form C. 2118.

Place	Date	Hour	Summary of Events and Information	Remarks and references to Appendices
			Brigade and were unable to move until daybreak. No change occurred during the night, whilst parties quietly in the forward area built their was a fair amount of shelling round Battalion Headquarters and behind, enemy using much gas. Casualties to Battalion were 112 of which 8 were killed, 73 wounded, and missing, 20 missing and 10 such. Captain A Forbes commdg No 3 Coy was wounded in the back about 7 P.M. and had to be evacuated. After having been excellent work with his Company. The enemy though not in great strength fought stubbornly and proved very difficult to drive off as there was no Artillery Support of any sort during the attack.	
	5th		The policy to-day was to reorganise in depth, having the enemy as much as possible and to push forward patrols. This was done and the day passed without much incident that touch was gained with the "New Zealand" Brigade for the first time in 24 hours. At night the Battalion was relieved by	

WAR DIARY
or
INTELLIGENCE SUMMARY.
(Erase heading not required.)

Army Form C. 2118.

Place	Date	Hour	Summary of Events and Information	Remarks and references to Appendices
	6th		8th Lincoln Regt. 63rd Inf. Bde. and proceeded to position in readiness in J.26.b. Move being complete about 5am 6th. Lieut Col J.T. HESELTON. D.S.O., M.C. WORCESTER REGT. assumed command of Bn. Bn. rested, reorganised Platoons & Sections and reconnitred defences which the Bn. had to man in the event of the Bn. line being driven in.	
	7th		2nd Bn. was attached to 63rd Infantry Brigade for current purpose and at 5.30 p.m. moved to position to Sunken road in P.3.a.	
	8th		No change in location.	
	9th		Battalion moved to Sunken Road J.36.c in close Support to 63rd Inf Bde.	
	11th		Bn. came under orders of 112th Inf. Bde. again at 10 p.m.	

Army Form C. 2118.

WAR DIARY
or
INTELLIGENCE SUMMARY.
(Erase heading not required.)

Instructions regarding War Diaries and Intelligence Summaries are contained in F. S. Regs., Part II and the Staff Manual respectively. Title pages will be prepared in manuscript.

Place	Date	Hour	Summary of Events and Information	Remarks and references to Appendices
	12th		Bn was placed at disposal of 111th Inf Bde, New Zealand Division, 111th Inf Bde and 63rd Division attacked at 5.25 am. Weather wet, especially in morning.	
	15th	5.0 am	Bn was called on by G.O.C. 63rd Inf Bde to send up two Coys as it was expected that the Enemy would attack.	
		6 am	Nos 1, 2 Coys moved up. During night 15/16th Bn relieved 5th Duke of Wellington's Regt in left Sub-Sector of 112th Bde front. Relief completed 1.5 am.	
	18th	5.15 am	After an intense barrage the enemy attacked our positions and after hard fighting gained a footing in our advanced posts, the enemy was later successfully driven back to his own lines leaving 26 unwounded prisoners in our hands.	
	19th		Bn relieved by 4th Middlesex Regt. at 9.30 pm and on relief	

WAR DIARY
or
INTELLIGENCE SUMMARY.

Army Form C. 2118.

Place	Date	Hour	Summary of Events and Information	Remarks and references to Appendices
	21st		moved to positions in main line of resistance. Bn relieved by 1/5th Manchester Regt and marched to beetle and huntments at BEUGNY	
	22nd		Bn marched back to a camp situated on the outskirts of WARLENCOURT	
	23rd to 28th		Time spent in reorganising and re-equipping the Battalion	
	29th		At 8 am the Bn moved to a camp situated on the FREMICOURT - LEBUCQUIERE road - accommodation poor.	
	30th		Bn moved to trenches near GOUZEACOURT in Divisional Reserve	
			During the month the following decorations were awarded to the undermentioned Officers, NCO's and men	

WAR DIARY
or
INTELLIGENCE SUMMARY.

Army Form C. 2118.

THE MILITARY CROSS.

2/Lieut. F.W. CRAKE.
2/Lieut. R.G. MORRISON.
2/Lieut. D. KEW. D.C.M., M.M.
Capt. P.W. Mac LAGAN. R.A.M.C. attached.

THE DISTINGUISHED CONDUCT MEDAL.

43127. Serg.t KING. T.H.

THE MILITARY MEDAL.

No 18826 Pte E. Bolahann
No 15646 Pte W.G. Barlow
No 266482 Pte B. Joad
No 270663 Pte F. Sanderson
No 285063 Pte T.A. Balch. D.C.M.

WAR DIARY
or
INTELLIGENCE SUMMARY.

(Erase heading not required.)

Army Form C. 2118.

Place	Date	Hour	Summary of Events and Information	Remarks and references to Appendices
			N° 42277 Pte. A. E. WARNE.	
			N° 40618 Pte. H. CLARKE.	
			N° 12349 Cpl. A. A. WRIGHT.	
			N° 1204 Pte. H. H. ALLEN.	
			N° 285016 Cpl. T. A. SMITH.	
			N° 265069 Pte. (A/L.Cpl.) F. T. RUDDOCK.	
			J. Smith	
			Lieut. Col.	
			Commanding 1st Bn. Hertfordshire Regiment	

Volume 98

War Diary
of
1st. Bn. The Hertfordshire Regiment
for the month
of
October 1918.

Army Form C. 2118.

WAR DIARY
or
INTELLIGENCE SUMMARY.
(Erase heading not required.)

Place	Date	Hour	Summary of Events and Information	Remarks and references to Appendices
October 1918.	1st		The Battalion moved to trenches at DEAD MANS CORNER.	
	2nd		Bn. moved into trenches at Q.29.a.B (Sheet 57.c)	
	8th		Bn. assembled at 04.00 hours, No 2 Company on LEFT, No 1 Coy on right with Nos 3 & 4 Coys in Support. The Bn moved forward at Zero hr plus 68. Nos 1,2 Coys crossed the Green line under our barage. No 1 Coy Encountered opposition from Machine Guns on the right flank but a Section of trench mortars silenced these after firing a few rounds. The Company then continued to advance and occupied the dotted Green line along the South side of BRISEUX WOOD. At 07.40 hours, No 2 Coy on the left was held up by machine gun fire from the Chateau and sustained several casualties. No 3 Coy was pushed forward to assist No 2 and together they cleared the Wood, South end	

Army Form C. 2118.

WAR DIARY
or
INTELLIGENCE SUMMARY.
(Erase heading not required.)

2

Place	Date	Hour	Summary of Events and Information	Remarks and references to Appendices
			not to arrived with units on LEFT. So patrols were sent out and it was found that the Right flank of the Middlesex Regt. was resting on the Chateau in N.10.C. – A platoon from No 3 Coy was sent up to gain touch and join up the line from the N.E. corner of BRISEUX WOOD to the right of the 4th Middlesex Regt. Coys dug in on this line and at 13.00 hrs handed over the green dotted line to the 4th Bn. Middlesex Regt. and withdrew to the GREEN LINE.	
	9th		The advance was resumed at 5.20 hours. The Battalion was on the right with 1st Essex on left. No 4 Coy right front, No 3 Coy left front, No 1, 2 Right and Left support Coys respectively. No opposition was encountered and the Bn. pushed forward and secured the objective with practically no casualties. The Battalion then returned W of LIGNY and pushed forward towards CAUDRY. It was found however that the Enemy were	

WAR DIARY
or
INTELLIGENCE SUMMARY.
(Erase heading not required.)

Army Form C. 2118.

Instructions regarding War Diaries and Intelligence Summaries are contained in F. S. Regs., Part II. and the Staff Manual respectively. Title pages will be prepared in manuscript.

Place	Date	Hour	Summary of Events and Information	Remarks and references to Appendices
			Taking the Western side of the village and the Bn. came under heavy machine gun and 77 m.m. fire from the railway. Several attempts were made to push forward but all attempts to dislodge the enemy failed. Orders were then received from 112th Bde to dig in on a line running through 1.29.c - 1.35.a+c and remain there for the night	
	10th		At dawn patrols were pushed forward and occupied the town of CAUDRY. The Bn. then pushed forward and occupied a line from J.15.c.4.7 (?) J.21.B.5.5. Companies dug in in this position and remained there during the day.	
	19th		The Bn. was attached to 63rd Brigade. During the morning two companies were attached to 8th Somerset L.I. and went forward to mop up the railway and to form a defensive flank.	

WAR DIARY
or
INTELLIGENCE SUMMARY.
(Erase heading not required.)

Army Form C. 2118.

Place	Date	Hour	Summary of Events and Information	Remarks and references to Appendices
	13th		The Battalion were withdrawn and on actual marches to billets in the town of CAUDRY. - Good billets for all.	
	16th		The G.O.C. 112th Bde addressed the Bn. during the morning	
	17th		The G.O.C. 37th Division inspected the Bn. during the morning	
	23rd		The Bn left CAUDRY and marched to BEAURAIN. Shortly after arrival the Bn. received orders to move up to assembly positions, arriving there at 3hrs. him on Oct 24th.	
	24th		The attack commenced at 04.00 hours. The barrage was good. The life Coy into very stiff opposition and gained the village of GAISSIGNIES at 11.00 hours. The right Coy were	

WAR DIARY
or
INTELLIGENCE SUMMARY.
(Erase heading not required.)

Army Form C. 2118.

Place	Date	Hour	Summary of Events and Information	Remarks and references to Appendices
			The Division on our right went forward and took road running S.E. through X.11.a.6.6 - X.17.B and gained touch with our right Coy at the HALT X.11.a.6.6. After a 1 minute barrage another attempt was made to gain the line of the railway, at 2.00 hrs. The two leading Coys crept forward under the barrage opened and at zero plus 1 rushed the railway. The enemy however who were holding the line strongly, opened heavy machine gun fire and inflicted many casualties. The two leading Coys were forced to withdraw again to the line of the road.	
	25th	At 10.00 hours, after a bombardment by 6" Newtons another attempt was made to take the railway. The right Coy took M.G. post and 1 prisoner but were forced to retire owing to heavy enfilade machine gun fire from both right and left flanks and heavy fire from trench mortars.	

WAR DIARY
or
INTELLIGENCE SUMMARY.
(Erase heading not required.)

Army Form C. 2118.

held up at first by Enemy machine guns but these were mopped up by the right support Coy. The leading Coy then advanced along the railway, enfiladed SALESCHES Station, about 50 Germans, 1 8" Howitzer and several machine guns. Heavy fighting took place all along the railway. The support Coy found a defensive flank facing S.E. as the Division on our right was held up. Several thousand yards in rear of our right flank. The leading Coy then pushed forward again to the line of road running through X.11.A. At this point heavy Machine gun fire was encountered from X.5.c.9.5. and from orchards in X.11.D. The left Coy was held up by M.G's. from X.5.a.5.4 and close in X.6 and X.5.A. Several attempts were made to gain the line of the railway by the M.G. fire was too heavy and a line of the road through X.4.a - X.5.c - X.11.d was established with posts in orchards 100 yards in front. At 17.00 hrs.

WAR DIARY
or
INTELLIGENCE SUMMARY.
(Erase heading not required.)

Army Form C. 2118.

Place	Date	Hour	Summary of Events and Information	Remarks and references to Appendices
	26th		Bn heavily shelled with gas shell – very uncomfortable.	
	27th		Bn relieved by 8th Bn Lincolns and moved to bivouacs near SALESCHES.	
	28th		Bn relieved by Bn K.R.R.C. and moved to billets in BEAUVRAIN – the whole Bn billeted in one large farm.	
	30th		Still at BEAUVRAIN.	

Honours & Rewards – overleaf.

WAR DIARY
or
INTELLIGENCE SUMMARY.

(Erase heading not required.)

Army Form C. 2118.

8

Place	Date	Hour	Summary of Events and Information	Remarks and references to Appendices
			During the month the following Awards were announced.	
			The Military Cross	
			Capt. P.H. Warbagan. R.A.M.C. Attd.	
			2/Lieut. D. Kew. D.C.M. M.M.	
			Lieut. M.a.B. Owen	
			2/Lieut. A.L. Allen	
			Bar to the Military Cross	
			2/Lieut. D. Kew. D.C.M. M.M.	
			P.T.O.	

WAR DIARY
or
INTELLIGENCE SUMMARY

Army Form C. 2118.

Summary of Events and Information

The Distinguished Conduct Medal.

4327 Sgt. T.H. King.
283016 Cpl. T.A. Smith.

The Military Medal.

20248	Pte	W. Bygraves		41015	Pte	W. Pinfold
335186	„	F. Arnold		17502	Sig	J.R. Logan
203549	„	A.S. Turvey		40686	Pte	J.A. Hargraves
291544	L/C	F.T. Cott		41444	Pte	H. Jooks
266506	„	J.R. Gough		16103	Pte	H. Bowles
26772	Cpl	R.E. Weaver		266106	L/Cpl	W. Granville
43164	L/Cpl	A.H. Long		13292	Cpl	T. Garment
265845	Pte	H.G. Winter		12653	Pte	E. Hebden
42023	Pte	B. Everard		304241	Sgt	C.W. Taylor
				19846	Cpl	E.A. Kaie

Army Form C. 2118.

WAR DIARY
or
INTELLIGENCE SUMMARY.
(Erase heading not required.)

Instructions regarding War Diaries and Intelligence Summaries are contained in F. S. Regs., Part II. and the Staff Manual respectively. Title pages will be prepared in manuscript.

Place	Date	Hour	Summary of Events and Information	Remarks and references to Appendices
			Bar to the Military Medal	
			Nº 10646. Pte. W.E. Barlow. M.M.	
			Nº 12349 Sig. J.J. W. Stanley. M.M.	
			Nº 265272 Sgt. R.L. Blakeley. M.M.	
	31.10.18			

J. Newton
Lieut. Col.
Commanding 1st. Battalion The Hertfordshire Regiment

Confidential

War Diary

of

1st Bn. The Hertfordshire Regt

for

November 1918

Army Form C. 2118.

WAR DIARY
or
INTELLIGENCE SUMMARY
(Erase heading not required.)

Place	Date	Hour	Summary of Events and Information	Remarks and references to Appendices
November 1st	3rd		Battalion resting at BEAURAIN.	
		17:30	At 17:30 hours the Battalion moved from billets in BEAURAIN to a position in readiness at BERNIER FARM. Accommodation was not good but luckily it was possible to get most of the men under cover until 04:00 hours on November 4th.	
	4th	06:00	At 06:00 hours the 111th Bde attacked the enemy's positions between the villages of GHISSIGNIES and LOUVIGNIES after a short but violent artillery preparation. Strong opposition was encountered on the Railway embankment in X5a2c, but this was overcome. Pushing on, the 111th Bde captured LOUVIGNIES and reached its final objective about 300 yds E of the PONT A VACHE, from which line the 112th Bde were to resume the attack. At 06:15 hours the Battalion moved forward, reaching the village of LOUVIGNIES at 08:00 hours and passed through the 111th Bde at 09:17 hours, resuming the attack under an artillery barrage with the 1st ESSEX on the left. No 4 Company was in reserve. The attack progressed favourably until the	

WAR DIARY
or
INTELLIGENCE SUMMARY
(Erase heading not required.)

Army Form C. 2118.

Place	Date	Hour	Summary of Events and Information	Remarks and references to Appendices
			stream and orchards in S9 b & S 10 c were reached. At this juncture the left Bn and Nos 2 & 3 Companies were held up by heavy MG fire. The nature of the country greatly favoured the defence, being very close, and therefore it was very difficult to locate the enemy. No 1 Company on the right however continued to advance, keeping in touch with the 17th Division. At about 12 hours the Lft Bn cleared the enemy machine guns and pushed forward, thus enabling our left Companies to resume the advance. At this point we captured 40 prisoners and several machine guns. The leading Companies passed through the village of JOLIMETZ and two oppositions was encountered until LAIECOULON was reached, although an extremely thin enemy barrage was put down in S 11 b & d. At this point strong enemy machine gun fire was opened out. This however lasted for only twenty minutes. At the end of which period the enemy retired. The Bn reached its final objective at 1500 hours. Later in the afternoon the 8th Somersets went through and advanced a considerable distance into the FORET DE MORMAL. About 100 prisoners were captured in JOLIMETZ and 5 77mm field guns in S 11 b & S 12 a.	

WAR DIARY
or
INTELLIGENCE SUMMARY

(Erase heading not required.)

Army Form C. 2118.

Place	Date	Hour	Summary of Events and Information	Remarks and references to Appendices
	5th		The Bn was withdrawn to GHISSIGNIES at 1000 hours. During this period the bodies of the men of this Bn who were killed in action in the attack of the 4th inst were recovered and buried at GHISSIGNIES.	
	11th		The Bn marched back to BETHENCOURT and remained therein training until Dec 1st '18. During this period Brigade Sports were held, this Bn being well represented. On the Divisional Football League the Bn won its first two matches, beating the 13th R.Bs. by 2 goals to 1 and Divisional Headquarters by 7 to 1 respectively.	
	21st		The 112th Inf. Bde was inspected by Major Gen. S.P. Williams C.B., D.S.O., Commanding 37th Divn.	
	22nd		The Bn marched to CAUDRY for Divisional Inspection by the Divisional Commander.	

During the month the following decorations were announced:-

<u>The Military Medal.</u>

12471. Cpl. R. Chambers.
269205 Sgt. J. Hickson.
37555 L/Cpl. G. Palmer.

The Military Medal (Contd)

33112 Sgt. S.C. Wilson.
32279 Pte. W.C. Davey.
265812 Sgt. L.G. Easton
42018 Pte. C. Caldwell.
42359 Sgt. E. Bowler.
32275 L/Cpl. J. Wells.
42444 Sgt. H.R. King.
32191. Cpl. F. Cutteridge.
266418 Pte. P. Bates.
28577 Pte. D.H. Frost.
45615 Pte. D. Todd.

J. Sheller
Lieut. Colonel.
Commanding 1st Bn. The Hertfordshire Regiment

SECRET

OPERATION ORDER No.6.

Reference Maps.
    51 S.W.) 1/20,000.   November 2nd.1918.
    51 A.S.E.)

1. The Battalion will be prepared to move to positions of assembly in K.M.d. and K.16.B and village of GHISSIGNIES at 17.00 hours to-morrow.

2. The Third Army is continuing the advance on Monday the 4th inst. The 37th Division are attacking the FORET MORMAL, objectives and Divisional boundaries on trace issued to O.C.Coys.

    At zero the 111th Brigade will advance under a creeping barrage and capture the dotted blue line.

    The 118th Brigade will pass through the 111th Brigade on dotted blue line at zero plus   and will capture the green line.

    Order of battle -
        1st.ESSEX REGT on LEFT.
        1st.HERTS.REGT on RIGHT.
        13th R.Fusiliers) Support.
        8th Somersets   )

    Inter Battalion Boundary - line running through S.3.C.5.5. to S.3.C.0.2. thence due EAST.
    The barrage will creep forward at the rate of 100 yards in six minutes.

                                  in line
    The Battalion will attack with 3 Coys.(each Coy.on 2 platoon frontage) and 1 in support. No.1 Coy.on RIGHT, No.3 Coy.in centre, No.2 Coy.on LEFT and No.4 Coy.in support. Liason posts with 1st.ESSEX will be established at the following points by No.3 Coy.-
        1. JOLIMETZ CHURCH S.4.C.7.7.
        2. S.5.C.3.1.
One platoon per leading Coy.will be detailed to "Mop up".

    On reaching the GREEN line the Battalion will halt for two hours to enable guns to be brought up. At zero plus the advance will be continued to the RED line where the 8th Battalion SOMERSET L.I. will pass through the leading Companies and continue the advance to the line of road in T.3.c and T.9.a.and c. Similarly the Royal Fusiliers will pass through the 1st.ESSEX

    General compass bearing of the advance is 101°

    Limbers will follow Coys.to assembly positions.

    Cookers will move forward to approx.K.M.d.7.7.

    Greatcoats will be carried rolled round the haversack.

    Fighting equipment will be drawn from Bn.H.Qrs.to-morrow,3rd.inst.

                                                      P.T.O.

In continuation of Operation Order No.6.

The attack will be carried out under an artillery, Trench Mortar and Machine Gun Barrage.

The Artillery barrage will open on black line at zero.

The Barrage will -

    Leave BLACK line at   zero plus 4 mins.
    " BLUE " "   zero " 110 "
    " Dotted Blue line at " " 197 "
    " Green Line for attack on left
    (Essex) at zero plus 342 min.
    " GREEN line for attack on right
    (Herts) at zero plus 449 min

The following pauses will be made in the barrage.

    ON BLUE LINE - 15 min.
    On DOTTED BLUE LINE - 30 "
    On GREEN LINE (left) - 12 "
    On GREEN LINE (right) - 2 hours.

The barrage will creep forward at a uniform rate of 100 yards in 6 minutes except that-

(a) The advance from the BLACK LINE to the BLUE LINE for the first 700 yards will be at 100 yards in 4 mins.

(b) The advance from the GREEN to the RED LINE (on left) will be at 100 yards in 4 mins.

The Battalion will leave the assembly positions in X.10.D., X.16.B. and GHISSIGNIES at zero plus 90.

The leading Companies will halt on ENGLEFONTAINE - LOUVIGNIES road in squares S.7.B.and D. until zero plus 180. Companies will then advance to dotted blue line, form up in S.9.A.and C. and be in readiness to pass through 111th Brigade at zero plus 197 mins.

On reaching the GREEN LINE Coys. will reorganize and halt for two hours. The advance to the RED line will be continued at zero plus 449.

On reaching RED line the 8th Battalion Somerset L.I. will leap-frog the leading Coys. and will exploit to RED dotted line.

In the event of the enemy retiring the advance will be pushed energetically on PONT SUR SAMBRE.

O.C.No. 4 Coy. Will establish liason post with 17th Division at cross roads S.17.a.65.75

Contact Aeroplane /

(2)

Contact Aeroplane will call for flares at

      zero plus 110.
         "   "   170.
         "   "   270.

and at intervals of two hours afterwards. In thick woods flares will also be lit in rides and clearings.

The General compass bearing of the advance will be 102° - magnetic.

Watches will be synchronised at Battalion H.Qrs. Farm BERNIER at 01.00 hours 4th Nov.

Artillery.

(a) During daylight smoke in the proportion of one round in 6 will be fired in the creeping barrage.

(b) Single Guns firing frontally will be employed firing THERMITE ahead of the barrage to mark the Divisional and Inter-Battalion boundaries.

3:11:18.

Captain & Adjt.,
1st.Bn.Hertfordshire Regiment.

(2)

Contact Aeroplane will call for flares at

zero plus 110.
  "   "   170.
  "   "   270.

and at intervals of two hours afterwards.
In thick woods flares will also be lit in rides and clearings.

The General compass bearing of the advance will be 102° - magnetic.

Watches will be synchronised at Battalion H.Qrs. Farm BERNIER at 01.00 hours 4th Nov.

Artillery.

(a) During daylight smoke in the proportion of one round in 6 will be fired in the creeping barrage.

(b) Single Guns firing frontally will be employed firing THERMITE ahead of the barrage to mark the Divisional and Inter-Battalion boundaries.

H.W. Goodson
Captain & Adjt.,
1st.Bn.Hertfordshire Regiment.

3:11:18.

CONFIDENTIAL

WAR DIARY

OF

1ST BATTN.

THE HERTFORDSHIRE REGT

FOR THE MONTH OF

DECEMBER 1918

Army Form C. 2118.

WAR DIARY
or
INTELLIGENCE SUMMARY.
(Erase heading not required.)

Instructions regarding War Diaries and Intelligence Summaries are contained in F. S. Regs., Part II. and the Staff Manual respectively. Title pages will be prepared in manuscript.

Place	Date	Hour	Summary of Events and Information	Remarks and references to Appendices
December 1st 1918			The Battalion marched to the village of VENDEGIES.	
	2nd		The Battalion marched to BRY and remained there until Dec. 14th. During this period spent at BRY inter-platoon football matches were played.	
	11th		The Battalion Colours, which had been deposited in All Saints Church, Retford, since August 1914 arrived from England in charge of the Colour Party which proceeded to England for them.	
	14th		The Battalion marched to BELLIGNIES.	
	15th		The Battalion marched to LA LONGUEVILLE.	
	17th		The Battalion marched to MAUBEUGE, arriving in the town at 12 noon. All ranks had the opportunity of visiting places of interest.	
	18th		The Battalion marched to BINCHE — Everyone in good billets.	

WAR DIARY
or
INTELLIGENCE SUMMARY.
(Erase heading not required.)

Army Form C. 2118.

Place	Date	Hour	Summary of Events and Information	Remarks and references to Appendices
	19th.		The Battalion marched to TRAZEGNIES	
	20th.		The Battalion marched to RANSART, a village about 4 miles N.E. of Charleroi.	
	31st.		Battalion still at RANSART. Plenty of amusement and recreation is being afforded all ranks. Erelia Christmas Fare was provided for the men on the 25th. On Christmas morning the Br. Football team played 50th Field Ambulance (friendly match) - result, draw. During the afternoon the Hockey match. Officers versus Sergeants resulted in a win for the Officers, the final score being 4. G. 3. On December 10th notification was received that the late 2/Lieut. F.E. YOUNG had been posthumously awarded the Victoria Cross for conspicuous gallantry and devotion to duty, near HAVRINCOURT on November 18th.	

WAR DIARY
or
INTELLIGENCE SUMMARY.

(Erase heading not required.)

Army Form C. 2118.

Place	Date	Hour	Summary of Events and Information	Remarks and references to Appendices
			The following other awards were announced:-	
			The Distinguished Conduct Medal.	
			N° 265287 C.S.M. K. DAVY.	
			" 42414 Sgt. H.R. KING, M.M.	
			" 266335 Sgt. C.J. LING.	

J.S. [signature]
Lieut-Colonel,
Commanding 1st. Battalion The Hertfordshire Regiment.

RETURN SHEWING DECREASE IN STRENGTH for the month of December 1918.
_____

	Off.	O.R.
Strength of Battalion, 1st. December 1918...	38	848

Decrease during month:-
    (a) Demobilized:-   Off. O.R.
        Coalminers... ... ... - 21
        Pivotals ... ... - 2
        Long Service ... ... - 8
                                       31

    (b) Evacuated sick and struck
        off strength ... ... - 11

    (c) Other causes:-   O.R.
        To 1st.Bedford.R.   1
        " 118th.Bde.   1
        " 794 Area.Em.Coy.   1
                         3   3

Total decrease during month .... - 45   - 45

Strength of Battalion, 1st. January 1919.   40   878.

H. Woodson
for Capt adjt
Lieut-Col.,
9/1/19.
Commanding 1st. Battalion The Hertfordshire Regiment.

1/1st Bⁿ· Hertfordshire Regt.

War Diary.

Volume LI

January, 1919.

WAR DIARY.

January 1919.

Battalion still in billets at RANSART. Educational Classes have been formed and are well attended, much benefit being derived from the scheme. A Recreational room has been opened and in addition, a Battalion Canteen Park has been formed.

Physical drill is carried out daily and on January 23rd a Battalion Route march was carried out. Weekly trips to Waterloo and Brussels have been arranged for Officers and men.

The Demobilization Office has been opened twice weekly to enable men to find out their position. Considerable numbers have taken advantage of the opportunity.

Twenty seven men have been sworn in for the Regular Army. During the month the following awards were announced.

O.B.E.
J. Barber.
Major. J. Barber.
Quartermaster.

WAR DIARY
or
INTELLIGENCE SUMMARY.
(Erase heading not required.)

Army Form C. 2118.

Place	Date	Hour	Summary of Events and Information	Remarks and references to Appendices
			Bar to the Military Cross.	
			Captain. P. G. Gold. M.C.	
			Bt. T. a. W. George (A.C.D). 2/Lieut. E. I. G. Ingram MC (Killed).	
			The Military Cross.	
			Lieut. R. K. J. Rowley.	
			2/Lieut. A. J. Bailey.	
			The Distinguished Conduct Medal.	
			No 13089 Sgt. B. Farrow.	
			No 265497 Sgt. D. Kitt.	
			The Meritorious Service Medal.	
			265018 R.Q.M.S. Keener J. 266539 a/cpl. Randall. A.C.	
			265055 Sgt. G. Courtney. 43598. Pte. Bidder. T.	

Army Form C. 2118.

WAR DIARY
or
INTELLIGENCE SUMMARY.
(Erase heading not required.)

Place	Date	Hour	Summary of Events and Information	Remarks and references to Appendices
			Mentioned in Despatches.	
			T/Capt (A. Lt/Col.) R.E. Carthew. M.C. 27.12.18.	
			Br. Mr. & Major. J. Barber. T.D. 30.12.18.	
			A number of Officers and Other ranks have proceeded to England for Demobilization. A return shewing numbers who have left is attached herewith	

Aylmer Ogle
Major
Commanding 1st. Bn. Hertfordshire Regt.

Return shewing decrease in Strength for the month
   of January 1919.

Strength of Unit, 1st.Jan 1919.   40.   878.

Decrease during month :-
   (a) Demobilized :-   O.   O.R.
       Pivotals .....   1.   7.
       Long Service ..   1.   14.
       ~~Long Service..~~
       Watford Details.   1.
       Guarantee Letter)
                    Men) 1.   48.
       A.F.Z.56... ...   1.
       Releasable Groups. 6.   54.
       Regular Soldiers)
       with 2 or more   )   13
       years to complete)
                              ─────────
                              9.   138.

   (b) Evacuated Sick and   10.
       struck off strength

   (c) Other Causes...   3   9.   151.
                                ─────────
                                31   727
                                ═════════

CONFIDENTIAL

WAR DIARY

OF

1/1ST Bn THE HERTFORDSHIRE REGT.

FOR THE MONTH OF

FEBRUARY 1919

VOLUME 52

Headquarters,
112th Infantry Brigade.
_____

                    Herewith War Diary for the month
                          of February 1919.

                                        H Goodson Capt & adjt.
                                  for.Lieut-Colonel,
28th Feb.1919.   Comdg.1st.Bn.Hertfordshire Regt.
_____   _____

WAR DIARY

February 1919

Battalion still in billets at PANSART. The Education Classes have been well attended during the month. The Battalion Concert Party, formed last month, proved a success and drew large audiences at each performance.

Owing to bad weather it was impossible to play the league football matches arranged for the early part of the month. The Battalion team however played the 37th D.A.C. on Feb. 18th and the 37th R.A.S.C. on Feb. 21st, winning both matches by 9-1 and 3-nil goals respectively. The Battalion is now at the top of the Divisional Football League.

2nd. The Battalion attended a parade for the presentation of colours to two Battalions in the Division.

During the month a further number of Officers and Other ranks have proceeded to England for Demobilization. and a number of horses and mules have been sold by

Action in the neighbouring district.
A return shewing number of Officers and Other
ranks who have proceeded to England for Demobilisation
is attached.

28th Feb. 1919.

J. Sewell
Lieut. Colonel.
Commanding 1st Bn. Bedfordshire Regiment.

Return shewing decrease in Strength for the month of February 1919.

Strength of Unit, 1st.Feb.1919.   31   727.

Decrease during month :-
(a) Demobilized :-   O.   O.R.
        Pivotals   1   5
        Long Service ..   -   24
        Watford Details..   -   -
        Guarantee Letter)   1   72
             Men   )
        A.F.Z.56 ... ..   -   2
        Releasable Groups.   -   74
        Serving Soldiers.   -   1
        Group 43   1   -
        Group 45.b. ..   1   -
                                ___   ____
                                 4   178.
(b) Evacuated Sick and
    struck off strength   13
                                 ___   ____
                                 4   191

    From Hospital etc..   -   5   4   186.
                                                    ___   ____

                Total Strength on 28/2/19.=   27   541

Army Form C. 2118.

WAR DIARY

INTELLIGENCE SUMMARY
(Erase heading not required.)

Instructions regarding War Diaries and Intelligence Summaries are contained in F.S. Regs., Part II. and the Staff Manual respectively. Title pages will be prepared in manuscript.

WO 153

Place	Date	Hour	Summary of Events and Information	Remarks and references to Appendices
RANSART.	1/3/19.		Battn in Billets at RANSART.	
	2/3/19		All available releasable personnel despatched to 4th Corps Concentration Camp for demobilization	
	3/3/19		Battn. reorganized into two Companies.	
	7/3/19.		Lt. Col. Hamilton DSO MC proceeded to England. Major A.G. Clark DSO MC assumed Command of the Battalion	
	10/3/19		Division Concentrated in Jumet area. Battn moved to Jumet at 14.30 hrs.	
Jumet.	11/3/19 to 31/3/19.		Battn in Billets at Jumet. Billets Good. Lt. GHYCUBEY MC + 27 B.V.A TENANT proceeded to Eng for demobilization 27/3/19.	

Sydney Clark
Major
Commanding 1st Battn The Hertfordshire Regt.

www.ingramcontent.com/pod-product-compliance
Lightning Source LLC
Chambersburg PA
CBHW081242170426
43191CB00034B/2017